CARMELO ANTHONY

IT'S JUST THE
BEGINNING

Positively for Kids®
Kirkland Avenue Office Park
811 Kirkland Avenue, Suite 200
Kirkland, WA 98033
www.positivelyforkids.com

Anthony, Carmelo, 1984-
Carmelo Anthony—It's Just the Beginning / by Carmelo Anthony with Greg Brown.
48 p. : ill. (mostly col.), ports. ; 26 cm. (Positively For Kids)

Summary: Denver Nuggets' rookie phenomenon, Carmelo Anthony, tells how he overcame the
hardships of growing up in the rough streets of Baltimore to become a successful college basketball
player and one of the youngest players in the NBA.
Audience: Grades 4-8

ISBN 0-9634650-7-4

1. Anthony, Carmelo, 1984- . Juvenile literature. 2. Basketball players—United States—
Juvenile literature. [1. Anthony, Carmelo, 1984-. 2. Basketball players—Biography.]
I. Brown, Greg, 1957-. II. Title.

796.323/092—dc21 [B]

Library of Congress Control Number:
2004110333

Photo Credits:
All photos courtesy of Carmelo Anthony and family except the following:
AP/Wide World: Cover; 29 left; 37 bottom; 42 middle. Steve Bowen: 26 left. Curtis A. Brown: 14 right;
15; 16. Andrew D. Bernstein: 34. Darrell Corbett: 14 left; 19; 21. Andy Cross/The Denver Post: 43. Charlie
Meyers/The Denver Post: 41 left. Getty Images: 24. Al Bello/Getty Images: 7. Craig Jones/Getty Images:
30; 33 top left; 33 top right; 33 bottom left; 33 middle left. Sabrina Hartel: 8 right; 9 left; 9 middle. Vito
Kwan: 8 middle; 13. Dick Thomas/ Les Schwab Invitational: 26 left; 27. NBAE: 25. Brian Bahr/NBAE/
Getty Images: 37 top. Nathaniel S. Butler/NBAE/Getty Images: 36 left. Jesse D. Garrabrant/NBAE/Getty
Images: 36 right; 42 left. Allen Einstein/NBAE/Getty Images: 40 left. Garrett Ellwood/NBAE/Getty Im-
ages: 5; 41 right. Kent Horner/NBAE/Getty Images: 45. David Sherman/NBAE/Getty Images: 40 right;
42 right. Jamie Squire/NBAE/Getty Images: 38; 39. Dennis Nett/The Post-Standard: 33 bottom right.
Michael A. Schwarz: 28.

Special Thanks:
Positively For Kids would like to thank the people and organizations that helped make this
book possible: Carmelo Anthony, his family and friends; Bill Sanders and Jane Yin of BDA Sports
Management; and the Denver Nuggets.

Book Design:
Methodologie, Inc., Seattle

Printed in Canada

CARMELO ANTHONY

IT'S JUST THE *BEGINNING*

BY CARMELO ANTHONY
WITH GREG BROWN

A POSITIVELY FOR KIDS BOOK

What's up?
I'm Carmelo Anthony.

It sounds crazy, I know, to write a book about my life before I turn 21. But so much has happened to me so quickly, I sometimes feel like I'm 30. There's a lot to tell.

Growing up in the rough streets of Brooklyn and Baltimore, I've seen things no child should see.

Not many of my homeboys would have predicted I'd play in the NBA. Back in the day, between ages 6-13, I had trouble just breathing, let alone running up and down a court.

Asthma squeezed my lungs glove-tight. My asthma attacks bounced me in and out of the hospital a couple times a month.

I caught the eyes of many on the court, sure enough, but I stood just 6 feet in 10th grade. It took a growth spurt of 5 inches in one year to put me above the pack.

Like Michael Jordan, I was cut from my high school varsity basketball team. For real!

YEAR **2004**

YEAR 1988

People in Denver know me by my smile. There were times, however, when I felt the whole world was against me. I'd ask, "Why me? Why did my father die? Why do I have to struggle so much?"

I lived in depressed places, and I've felt depression. My biggest goal growing up was surviving.

I almost dropped the ball and walked away from basketball in high school. I cut classes and practices. My grades fell. I didn't care.

I finally made some serious changes and took control of my life. I'm the first in my family to go to college.

As a freshman, I helped Syracuse University win an NCAA basketball title. When Denver drafted me, I became an instant millionaire, a few years after washing car windshields for donations. My rookie year, the Nuggets made the playoffs for the first time in nine years.

I've written this book to share with you my life story because people go through rough times. I'm here to say stay strong. Today is a new chance. It's just the beginning.

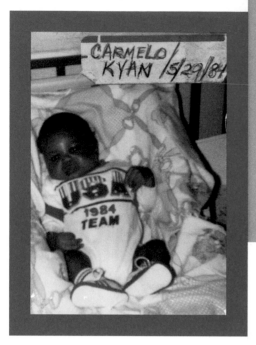

> Somebody had a feeling I would play for Team USA when I was born.

> These four middle pictures show the Red Hook projects where I grew up. Right there is the basketball court I first learned to play basketball and the courtyard where I played.

My beginning started in Brooklyn, New York, in a place called the Red Hook projects. The public housing was built in the 1930s on a peninsula. The 12-block area is cut off from the world because there is no subway. The isolation makes the 6- to 14-story brick buildings more like prisons than apartments.

We lived in a three-room apartment on Lorraine Street on the first floor. I was the baby of the family, which included two brothers and a sister. My father, Carmelo, was Puerto Rican, but I never got to know him. He died of cancer when I was 2.

My brothers and sister are all older than me. I grew up tagging along with them. I always wanted to follow in their footsteps. The neighborhood was rough, but I felt safe. We had a big extended family and everyone looked after me.

From our windows, you could see a basketball court where players gathered daily. My brother Wilford, now that he could play some hoops, would play all the time.

I wanted to watch him from the window; one day, when I was about 3, a stereo speaker blocked my view. I tried to climb the speakers three times.

> Mom had me stylin' in a toddler suit.

I had tried it before and my mom told me not to do it again. I did it again and got caught. Some time later I tried a third time. I fell and cut my eye. The gash needed stitches, but we didn't get them and you can still see the scar today. It was the first of many lessons I learned the hard way.

While I always wanted to watch Wilford play, I didn't study his moves or anything like that. I wasn't a student of basketball. It was just something fun to do.

I did love riding my bike around when I got older. If I wasn't riding my BMX bike around, I was outside playing on the monkey bars or something. I just never wanted to come inside. I always feared somebody would jack my bike, but it never happened. I did have my most precious piece of jewelry ripped off, right from my neck. Mom gave me this gold chain with Jesus on the cross. It used to be my dad's. So I'd wear it around to feel connected to him. A friend of my brother eyed it one day and snatched it right from my neck. I was still young, 5 or 6. I raced home and told Mom and my brother about it. When they cornered him about it, he lied to their faces, saying he didn't do it. To this day he still says he didn't do it. And to this day I still don't have my dad's cross and chain.

That was the most hurtful thing that happened to me at the Red Hooks.

Considering the neighborhood, I got off pretty easy. One of the best things I remember about Brooklyn is winning a trophy in my first basketball tournament.

EVERY SUMMER A BASKETBALL TOURNAMENT IS PLAYED ON THE CONCRETE COURTS AT THE RED HOOKS. THEY CALL IT THE PARADISE CLASSIC.

They had a younger division, 7–12 year olds, and an older division. When I turned 7, I wanted to play. Everyone in the projects watched the games.

I must have done something right because I received a trophy for being the Most Valuable Player of the tournament. At the time I didn't know better. I thought everyone got a trophy. Looking back, getting the MVP at 7 is pretty good.

> **Mom (left), who has been there for me from the beginning, celebrates with me and my sister Michelle.**

Just running up and down the court seemed miraculous to me. That's because summers brought bouts of asthma. My throat and lungs would constrict and, at times, I struggled to breathe normally thanks to allergies.

It got so bad, Mom would rush me to the hospital where I spent up to five days in oxygen tents or linked up to oxygen bottles. I'd push these oxygen stands around the hallways, with an IV in my arm, trying to breathe and talk to people.

"What's shakin,' Jello?"

Besides calling me "Melo," my family and friends used to call me "Jello." Doctors and nurses got to know me.

For a stretch, I needed the hospital treatments a couple times a month. I missed some school, but many times it happened on Fridays and it would wreck the weekend. I wasn't deathly afraid of my attacks, but they made me think.

I'd start coughing real hard. I had these pills that helped some. Then I'd start breathing real heavy. Then I'd get anxious and the cycle would repeat and get worse and worse. Sometimes I couldn't sleep. The day would be fine and it would come on like a storm. I'd get hyped and end up in the hospital.

My hospital stays started me worrying about surviving. I wanted to survive. Once I turned 13, the asthma suddenly went away.

> I'm on the far left in this team picture along with Coach Darrell Corbett, my longtime youth coach who had a big impact on my life.

Our family move might have had something to do with my recovery. When I was in third grade, Mom decided to move us to Baltimore.

"Why are we going?" I cried and cried.

Mom said she was tired of New York, and wanted to try something new.

I didn't want to go. My brothers were old enough to live on their own. They decided they didn't want to go either and went their own way. Mom took just my sister and me.

Oh, yeah, it was tough. I had tight friends, and I enjoyed school. I hated telling all my friends I had to leave.

MAKING NEW FRIENDS WAS DEFINITELY HARD. I WENT FROM ONE ROUGH 'HOOD TO ANOTHER. IN BOTH PLACES I SAW MANY TERRIBLE THINGS.

Street-corner drug dealing, prostitution, gangs, armed robberies, violence, and murder were all around me. I saw my first deadly shooting when I was 10. It happened 50 feet away in the street.

It was pretty stressful, at first, to meet new people. I mean, in Baltimore, you really had to fight your way to have a name out there. I never got jumped by a gang. But guys would challenge you one-on-one in the street. People came up to you and gave you lip. You try to ignore it, but it's hard. I had my share of scuffles. People would test you, and you have to make your mark. Everyone who comes into the neighborhood had to go through it.

> **Mount Royal Recreation Center is a place I used to play a lot of hoops. The other scenes are from my 'hood in Baltimore: a neighborhood street, my front door, and a nearby store.**

I remember one kid asked me where I was from when I first arrived in Baltimore. I said I was from New York. He was like, "You can't live around here." I mean these were young guys talking trash.

I noticed people had trouble saying Carmelo, because it's a Puerto Rican name. On my first day of school I told everyone, including teachers, that my name was Tyrone. So everyone, I'm talking the whole school, called me Tyrone for about a month.

School administrators found out my real name from records, and I got in big trouble. It wouldn't be the last time.

From then on, my elementary school days went smoothly. I loved school. I loved making people laugh too. I guess you could say I was the class clown at times.

I never played a musical instrument or performed in a talent show, but one of my talents is being a great speller. As punishment for goofing around, my teachers would make me stand in front of the class and spell a word. I would spell back the biggest words perfectly, and my teacher got flustered because she couldn't stump me. After a while, they put me in school spelling competitions and I won four or five trophies. I used to love spelling words for people.

Some have to study words over and over. I'm not like that. I would just see the word once, and bam, I'd get it.

When I can look at something, and take a picture of it in my mind, I can remember it. I didn't have to read books over and over to remember them. I enjoyed writing. Sometimes I wrote fiction stories just for fun—scary stuff. I'd draw pictures, too.

I also liked math. I loved the challenge of getting the answer. I enjoyed thinking of the different ways to get the same answer. In college, there were a lot of classes I didn't want to take, but I didn't care how early I had to get up for my math class.

History is one subject I didn't get into much. The thing that confused me was hearing teachers explain the same world events differently. I didn't know which version to believe.

Besides basketball, I showed some talent in other sports. I played some youth football. I was pretty good. They put me at quarterback and runningback. If basketball didn't work out, my dream would've been to play baseball. I loved playing baseball during elementary school.

I played first base and I pitched. My best baseball memory is hitting a home run in fourth grade. I hit it off the best pitcher in the area, a guy I played a lot of basketball with, Darnell Hopkins. I jacked a towering homer over this gate in the outfield. It felt so sweet. I was like, "How'd I do that?"

To this day we talk about it when we see each other.

"Remember that home run I hit off you?" I'll say.

"Yeah, I remember, my arm was hurtin' that day," he'll say.

Believe it or not, I didn't dream of playing in the NBA. You hear coaches say how only one in a million players makes it. They always said we needed a backup plan in case we didn't make it to the top. Education is a great Plan B for an athlete. With those odds, I didn't dare to think about the pros. I never thought basketball would take me as far as it has. I just played basketball for the fun of it and the challenge. Even back then, the better the competition, the better I did.

I started with AAU basketball in elementary school. I took my first flight at 9 when I traveled to an AAU tournament in Florida. I didn't take basketball seriously until high school. I didn't take a lot of things seriously. I was a last-minute person.

I didn't drop that first Florida trip on my mom until it got close. That's because I knew she'd say no. I had two players come sleep over when I finally told her about it two days before we were supposed to go. I thought they could talk her into it.

"You ain't goin' nowhere." Mom said.

I begged and pouted. I needed my coach to call her before she finally gave in. With all the summer traveling around for the AAU tournaments, money became a problem. We were always having raffles and fund-raisers for the team and my own fund. Mom worked as a housekeeper at the University of Baltimore.

I HAD TO HUSTLE A LITTLE ON THE STREET TO MAKE MONEY. I'D WASH CAR WINDOWS WHEN PEOPLE STOPPED ON STREET CORNERS OR PUMP GAS FOR PEOPLE WHEN THEY PULLED UP TO A GAS STATION.

Most people would give me a few bucks for my effort. It was fun. A friend and I made it a competition. I once earned $76 in one day. The experience taught me a lot about dealing with people. Some I came across were the biggest jerks. Others were so nice. It taught me to look at things from a different angle, that everyone is different.

I also made some change when everyone knew I was the basketball player in the neighborhood. People would come to my door and ask to play one-on-one.

When new people came through they always wanted to play the top guy. They'd say, "Come on, let's go play and see what you got."

Mom always said, "Don't you be playing for money, now." But I'd go out and play.

WHEN I HAD MONEY IN MY HAND, IT'D BE LIKE SAND. IT CAME AND WENT THROUGH MY FINGERS. I WAS KIND OF IRRESPONSIBLE.

I'd leave coats and other stuff just lying around and lose them. Mom worked hard for our money so that always got her boiling.

I'd get an allowance—about $10 a week in elementary school, $30 a week in junior high and $70 a week in high school. When I had money in my wallet, it would be gone in five minutes. At the end of the week I'd be broke. I was a big spender. I'd buy stupid stuff, things I didn't need.

For example, I remember once Mom gave me $100 to go get some shoes when I was 14. I thought I was the big man on the block. I spent it on cab rides, T-shirts, food, toys, and other dumb stuff. I never got the shoes though.

FUN FACT >>> CARMELO AVERAGED AS A SOPHOMORE 14.0 PPG, 5.0 RPG, 4.0 APG, 2.0 SPG, AND HELPED TOWNSON CATHOLIC TO A 26-3 RECORD AND A THIRD PLACE FINISH IN THE STATE CHAMPIONSHIP.

> I'm No. 23 ready to start a fastbreak in an AAU game.

> Our team stops for a picture during a road trip (I'm fourth down from the top).

> I score a layup in the Mount Royal gym.

NOW THAT I HAVE "SOME" MONEY, THE PROFESSIONAL PEOPLE AROUND ME ARE TEACHING ME THE VALUE OF HAVING A BUDGET AND STICKING TO IT.

You hear all those stories about athletes, stars, and rappers who blow through their cash and go broke. I was dead tight at first. Now I've loosened up. My budget tells me when to stop.

Mom put her foot down whenever anyone tried to give me money or gifts. I played a lot of hoops at the Mount Royal Recreation Center and my name was ringing a lot. College coaches and agents would come to scout older players and they noticed me, starting in junior high. Even though I wasn't that tall yet, I had some skills. I broke 6 feet in 10th grade.

So people would try to give me things. Mom would get so mad if I brought back clothes, or whatever. Mom's rule was if she couldn't afford it, it wasn't worth having. I swear, even if I came home with a pen, she'd say, "Take it back."

> I'm all smiles after receiving a Player of the Week award while playing for the Towson Catholic Owls.

First it was the recruiters, then the agents. Later on in high school, agents were hovering around my house all the time. I got fed up with it. I thought, "Let me be myself." Some would come into the neighborhood, rolling up with nice cars with TVs and my friends would be like, "Who's that?" The agents would try to treat my friends to get close to me.

Mom wisely knew better. She knew the dangers that lurked behind those gifts. She'd say the point is there is always something behind such gifts. If someone gave me something now, they'd want something in return later. She was right. I'm thankful I listened and didn't owe anyone. Besides, if you want to play college basketball, you can't take anything. I wanted to play in college.

My brother, Wilford, had a chance to play major college basketball. He had a lot of things going for him. He went to one of the best basketball high schools in New York—Boys and Girls High. Then he had a chance to go to a lot of different colleges, but he took the wrong route. The glitter of the street turned his head. It wasn't drugs, just the action. Wilford is doing fine, but he'll be the first to tell you he missed his chance.

Coming out of any street, it's hard to be alone. That was his problem. He didn't want to leave the streets.

I mean, I think I had that same problem growing up.

FUN FACT >>> AS A JUNIOR IN 2000-01, CARMELO AVERAGED 27.0 PPG, 8.0 RPG, 3.0 APG, AND HELPED LEAD TOWSON CATHOLIC HIGH SCHOOL TO A 23-6 RECORD AND A FOURTH PLACE FINISH IN THE STATE TOURNAMENT.

WE'D GO TO AAU TOURNAMENTS AND I'D BE HANGIN' OUT ON THE STREETS AND I WAS LIKE "FORGET THAT TOURNAMENT." I JUST WANTED TO STAY AND HANG OUT.

My coach would say, "You gotta come with us. You have to leave the streets."

It's been the hardest thing to give up—hanging out in the streets with my friends, especially in the summer months. It gets so dripping hot in the East, I always wanted to be outside to catch a breeze. It's not about drugs or gang stuff. I just liked being out. I could be sittin' on some steps or just walking up and down a street. It's reality TV right in front of your face.

Where I come from, being in the street is like being at home. Mom did a great job of raising me. She was always on me about things. I give her credit for everything I am. But I didn't have a father figure in my life for a long time. None of my friends had father figures either. So we became each other's role models. We looked up to ourselves and went to each other for answers. Most of the time that

> As you can see I looked like an average skinny player. I did have a big smile, even then.

worked. There are times, however, when you need a "father" to tell you straight up what's right and wrong. Someone to watch over you and give you advice.

If someone would have asked me at 8, 10, 12, 14, 16 years of age: "Carmelo, what's the one thing you want in the whole world?" At each of those ages I would've said the same thing.

"I want a father!"

If you have a father, even if he's not the greatest dad, there are millions of kids who pray each night for what you have.

Finally, just when I needed a male figure the most, one person stepped into my life and stepped up with his time.

Robert "Bay" Frasier was a Baltimore basketball freak. I'd seen him all around the gyms for a long time. He came around me my sophomore year in high school through another guy who went to school. I needed some direction.

MY FRESHMAN YEAR I WAS JUST MAD AT THE WORLD THE WHOLE YEAR. MOM DECIDED TO SEND ME TO TOWSON CATHOLIC SCHOOL.

Even though it was tough on us to pay the $7,000-a-year tuition, Mom wanted me to get a Christian education. Playing basketball had something to do with it as well. Towson was big on basketball at the time.

Still, I wanted to stay in my area and attend public school like the rest of my friends.

Towson wasn't close. I needed to take a commuter train ride and then a city bus. The commute took me about 40 minutes a day—each way. The school had mostly white students. It seemed like most of the blacks there played sports. I had to wear a uniform, khaki pants and a tie. Walking through my streets wasn't so bad. People understood and didn't give me a bad time. I did my best to make them look stylin'. I pulled out my shirt some and wore my pants low.

FUN FACT >>> CARMELO WAS NAMED THE 2001 BALTIMORE CITY AND COUNTY PLAYER OF THE YEAR, ALL-METROPOLITAN PLAYER OF THE YEAR AND BALTIMORE CATHOLIC LEAGUE PLAYER OF THE YEAR.

23

WHAT IS DEPRESSION?

Depression is more than the blues
Depression is not a personal weakness
Depression is a treatable illness

About Depression

Depression affects many young people and adults. About 1 in 12 adolescents suffer from major depression. Almost 1 in 10 adults feel depressed.

Depression has no single cause; often, it results from a combination of things. You may have no idea why depression has struck you. Factors include family history (it can be linked to genetics), trauma and stress, a negative outlook on life, medical conditions, or a chemical imbalance in the brain.

Symptoms of Depression

- constant feelings of sadness, irritability, or tension
- decreased interest or pleasure in usual activities or hobbies
- loss of energy, feeling tired despite lack of activity
- a change in appetite, with significant weight loss or weight gain
- a change in sleeping patterns, such as difficulty sleeping, early morning awakening, or sleeping too much
- restlessness or feeling slowed down
- decreased ability to make decisions or concentrate
- feelings of worthlessness, hopelessness, or guilt
- thoughts of suicide or death

Things to Remember

Depression can make you feel hopeless, afraid, and alone. It can make you feel like things will never get better. But once you find the right treatment, you can start to feel like yourself again.

- Depression is a medical condition and you are not to blame for it.
- Depression is treatable and most people who receive help get better.
- The first step to recovery is telling loved ones how you feel.
- The second step is willingness to talk to professionals and be open to various treatments.
- If you feel life isn't worth living, it's a symptom of depression, and you need to tell someone so you can get help immediately.

For Help or More Information Call:

National Youth Crisis Hotline 1.800.442.HOPE (4673)

On-line References

www.safeyouth.org
www.healthyplace.com
www.depression.com
www.teen-moods.net

That first year beat me down. The new adjustment took time. That winter it got worse. Basketball coach Mike Daniels brought two of us up on varsity. I was excited to play. Not many freshman play varsity in high school. He promised me that I would be on varsity and play a big role. Before the season started, Coach Daniels sat me down and said he had to send me back down to the junior varsity. I got cut! I walked out and didn't say anything to him for three months. I believed I could play up there.

That's when my whole thought process changed. I started thinking the whole world was against me. I had a negative view on things. If something good happened, I figured something bad was right around the corner. Maybe it was my environment. I didn't dare dream good things could happen to me. I'd always lament, "Why me? Why do I have to struggle and go through all of this?" Being cut took it to a darker level.

My grades were sorry in high school. I dipped below a C average my freshman year. In class, I had a problem with speaking out loud. I would just blurt out things. When the teacher asked a question, I'd just say the answer right as someone would raise a hand. So I'd get in trouble in class for speaking out. I'd be disruptive in the hallways, too. I like to dance. I'd dance in the halls, tryin' new moves, just tryin' to be funny.

Anger surfaced. I'd get chipped on. We had 3 minutes between classes. I'd get in trouble for being a minute early. I'd get in trouble for being 30 seconds late. If my shirt was out a bit, if my book bag was unzipped, if my locker wasn't locked, I'd get in trouble. When a teacher or administrator said something, my temper showed. "Why me? Why are you choosing me to target?"

There were days I thought, "I don't need this."

I simply lacked motivation. Sometimes I didn't go to school—just stayed home. I cut practices, too. I'd only show up for games. I learned the hard way. I always learn the hard way.

BAY, WHO'S ABOUT 10 YEARS OLDER THAN I AM, CAME ALONG MY SOPHOMORE YEAR. EVER SINCE THEN I'VE LOOKED UP TO HIM AS MY MALE FIGURE. HE PUT ME BACK ON THE RIGHT ROAD.

"You can't keep doin' this," he'd say.

"Man, I don't even want to play basketball anymore," I answered.

"Melo, you've got a future. Don't throw it away."

There were nights I didn't try on the court either. Coach Daniels once blasted me in front of the whole team, saying I was the worst defensive player he'd ever seen. Defense is about effort. I wasn't giving it. I was thinking, "Hey Coach, we're winning, so what?"

Against the worst team in our league, I had my worst high school game. I scored just two points. I missed layups and everything.

My sophomore year I buckled down some with Bay's prodding. That summer I went through the biggest growth spurt of my life—5 inches. I went from 6-1 to

> Here are my closest friends (from left to right) Tynell Dunkley, Tyler Smith, Kenneth Minor, Dontaye Draper, and Robert "Bay" Frazier.

6-6. It got to the point where my knees hurt and all my joints in my body hurt. It hurt to walk. I ate anything and everything and couldn't gain weight.

My added height gained me more respect on the court. My junior year I started taking the game seriously. I announced on my 17th birthday that I'd play college basketball up in Syracuse, New York. I got so tired of the stream of coaches coming through, I wanted to get it over. Assistant coach Troy Weaver recruited me to the Orangemen, and didn't give me anything, either.

There was one problem with the early signing. I started slipping backwards my junior year. My grades went down from my sophomore year. Distractions were pulling me down.

Mom was so disappointed.

"I'm working so hard for this tuition money and this is how you repay me? What's wrong with you, child?"

Mom took matters into her own hands. She decided to send me to boarding school for my senior year.

"I have a school for you, Oak Hill Academy," she said.

"I'm not going down there." I said, even though I knew Oak Hill had been national high school champions the year before (they have won five).

"You're not staying up here. You're cutting classes and not trying. Yes, you are going!" Mom said. Oak Hill sent us the paperwork and it was settled.

Before I left, I went to Las Vegas for a tournament.

> **My teammates and me at Oak Hill Academy relax outside.**

> **I drive to the hoop my senior year.**

> As you can see, I've worn headbands all the way back to high school, and even before.

Until that summer, I didn't go to any big-time AAU tournaments or camps. I was always sitting in summer school getting my grades back up so I could play basketball. Before my senior year started, our AAU team played in the Adidas Big Time Tournament in Las Vegas. I told my teammates, this is my time to shine. I went off. I scored a tournament record 230 points in eight games. I think it's still a record.

I WENT FROM BEING IN THE TOP 75 HIGH SCHOOL PLAYERS IN THE COUNTRY TO SOME SAYING I WAS THE NO. 1 PLAYER. I TOOK BASKETBALL MORE SERIOUSLY.

I did go to one camp—The ABCD camp in Patterson, New Jersey. I attended one day. I wanted to play this guy everyone was talkin' up—Lenny Cook. I left the camp after one day to go to summer school. I was so mad at myself.

I had to take summer classes at Oak Hill, about 390 miles south of Baltimore in remote Mouth of Wilson, Virginia. Mom dragged me down there at night. I couldn't see anything around. In the morning, I saw it was in the middle of nowhere. I called home every day saying, "I'm comin' home today!" That lasted about a month.

Then the school year started and they made me cut my hair and take out my cornrows. It was tough. I got used to it, though. The discipline was what I needed.

FUN FACT >>> AS A SENIOR IN 2001-02, CARMELO AVERAGED 22 PPG, 7.1 RPG, 3.0 APG, 1.8 SPG, AND SHOT 58.0 PERCENT FROM THE FLOOR, 48.0 PERCENT FROM 3-POINT, AND 68.0 PERCENT FROM THE FOUL LINE FOR OAK HILL ACADEMY.

27

That was probably the best thing that happened to me. Just getting to know myself better as a person, as an individual. Being able to mature on my own. I was truly focused on what I wanted to do.

I don't remember having a bad game for Oak Hill. We played an independent schedule and traveled all over the country. My best tournament, the Nike Extravaganza Tournament of Champions, we knocked out the defending champion and made it to the title game. I scored 30 points with 10 rebounds in the loss.

That wasn't my best game, though.

MY BEST GAME WAS AGAINST A JUNIOR NAMED LEBRON JAMES. MAYBE YOU'VE HEARD OF HIM. HE PLAYED FOR ST. VINCENT-ST. MARY. WE SQUARED OFF AND I HAD 34 POINTS AND 11 REBOUNDS, HE HAD 36 AND 9, BUT WE WON 72-66.

Graduating from Oak Hill made me the happiest man on earth. I went down there for school to get my grades right. At the end of months of intense work, I realized it was the best thing for me. Coming out of Baltimore I had a 1.9 GPA. Once I graduated I realized those six months were the best of my life. I got on top of my grades and on top of my game. My GPA went from a 1.9 to a 3.1.

The highlight of the year came when I heard about my ACT score. I took the SAT twice and failed, and took the ACT twice, failing the first time. I needed an 18 score on my ACT to be eligible for my college scholarship at Syracuse. It came down to my last try.

I was in history class one day, bored out of my mind. Then the office secretary, Lisa Smith, who happened to be basketball coach Steve Smith's wife, called me down to the office. She had this look on her face and told me to call my mother at home. I didn't know what was going on.

I called home and Mom was crying. "I'm so proud of you. You got your score!" she said.

I dropped the phone and ran into the hall. I yelled, "I got my score." People were high-fiving me as if I'd scored a game-winning basket. I got a 19. Made it to college by one point.

> I felt honored to play in the McDonald's Boys All-American game. I scored 19 as our East team beat the West 138-107.

FUN FACT >>> CARMELO WAS NAMED 2002 *USA TODAY* ALL-USA FIRST TEAM, *PARADE MAGAZINE* ALL-AMERICAN FIRST TEAM AND *BASKET-BALL AMERICA* ALL-AMERICAN FIRST TEAM.

29

Oak Hill prepared me well for Syracuse University, about a 5 1/2-hour drive north-east of Baltimore. Once I got to college, I was thinking this is what I want to do. This is where I want to be. The hardest adjustment was 7 a.m. basketball practices. Each player had individual sessions to work on drills. Mine was from 7-8 a.m. Coach Weaver sat me down and said I have a bright future and to get there I needed to make those early workouts.

"I can't get up at 7 in the morning. No way, man," I told him.

At 6:45 a.m. Coach Weaver would come to my apartment and pull the covers off me and start yelling: "Let's go work out. Come on! There are other people trying to take your spot and out-do you. They're working out right now."

I always got up and did the drills. But it was way too early to breathe hard.

Our 2003 Orangeman team was young. Eventually two freshman and two sopho-mores started. Nobody really knew what to expect. We were so doubted. We were ranked 65th at the beginning of the year.

We opened our season at Madison Square Garden in New York against Memphis. We lost. I scored 27 points, most in the first half. I faded in the second half.

COACH WEAVER AND I TALKED AFTER THE GAME. HE EXPLAINED HOW MUCH HARDER I'D HAVE TO WORK TO BE SUCCESSFUL AT THE COLLEGE LEVEL. THAT BECAME A TURNING POINT.

People started talking about us during a 12-game winning streak. We climbed to No. 12 in the national rankings and entered the NCAA tournament as the 3rd-seeded team in the Eastern region.

We shocked many "experts" by running the tournament table with six straight wins. We beat Manhattan, Oklahoma State, Auburn, and Oklahoma to advance to the Final Four in New Orleans. There we downed Texas by 11 in the semifinals, then upset second-ranked Kansas 81-78, to win the NCAA championship. It was the first time Syracuse won a men's NCAA basketball title.

I never felt so good about anything as I did right before the title game. We knew we weren't going to lose. I've been on winning teams my whole life. My teams won the elementary title, the middle school title, and my high schools won championships. Winning the NCAA title, that was the big one.

I loved the atmosphere of big-time college basketball and the great support of our fans. My year in college was invaluable. It taught me how to focus, how to stay prepared for everything. And it taught me patience. Sitting in class for 2 1/2 hours taught me a lot of patience.

Everyone thought it was a slam dunk that I'd leave school for the NBA after my freshman season. Head coach Jim Boeheim said after the season: "Melo, get your stuff and don't come back."

I HELD A PRESS CONFERENCE 17 DAYS AFTER THE CHAMPION-SHIP GAME. WOULD I STAY? WOULD I LEAVE? I WAS UNDECI-DED UNTIL 30 MINUTES BEFORE THE PRESS CONFERENCE. ALL MY TEAMMATES WERE THERE.

You build relationships with your teammates and you don't want to break up something good. They all encouraged me to take the next step and that made it a little easier.

"You gotta go," they said. "We won a championship. You can't stay."

Cleveland took LeBron in the first pick in the 2003 NBA draft. Detroit took 7-footer Darko Milicik No. 2. Denver picked me third.

FUN FACT >>> CARMELO USED TO GET IN TROUBLE AT SYRACUSE TEAM MEETINGS BECAUSE HE ALWAYS LIKES TO TAKE HIS SHIRT OFF WHEN IT'S THE LEAST BIT WARM OUTSIDE OR INSIDE.

I was cool with it. Detroit obviously didn't need me as they went on to stun the Los Angeles Lakers in the 2004 NBA Finals. I believe things happen for a reason. Denver needed me more.

The team had gone through some rough times. The Nuggets were 17-43 in 2003 and had not been to the playoffs since 1995. Everyone wondered how much I would help the team in my first year. I embraced Denver, and the city and Nuggets organization made me feel welcome.

Before the season started, I predicted to Denver reporters that we'd double our win total from the previous season and make it to the playoffs. Some snickered, as if to say, "He's young. He'll learn."

I looked forward to playing the Los Angeles Lakers the most.

ONE OF THE COOLEST THINGS ABOUT BEING IN THE NBA IS COMPETING AGAINST ALL THE BIG NAMES, THE PLAYERS YOU LOOKED UP TO GROWING UP.

Our first game against the Lakers we lost by 2 points in L.A., but Kobe Bryant didn't play. I felt proud I could come out and play against the guys I'd seen on TV. When I'm doing just as good as them, or better, my confidence goes sky high.

The second Laker game was in Denver. Kobe said he was looking forward to playing against me. I thought, "Yeah, bring it on." It was challenging on both ends of the court and we got into it. I started to do well and I thought, "Man, I guess I can play this game." Everybody looks up to Kobe on the court. I think he's the best player in the NBA right now. To be able to compete against him made me feel I belonged in the NBA. We beat LA the second time, 113-91 though. I finished with 20 points and 8 rebounds. Kobe had 27 points. The Lakers won the final two meetings, the last one by just a single point.

MY ROOKIE SEASON IN THE NBA HAD ITS UPS AND DOWNS. MAKING THE PLAYOFFS AND WINNING 43 REGULAR-SEASON GAMES WERE THE ULTIMATE HIGHLIGHTS.

The only game in my life where I've felt nervous was our first playoff game against Minnesota. I guess it didn't hurt me too much, as I scored 19 points in a 106-92 loss.

After a second loss, we came back in the third game to post a 107-86 win, but eventually lost the series 4-1. A big scare came in the fourth game when I landed awkwardly after a rebound and twisted my knee. It just wasn't my night, as I only made 1 of 16 shots and finished with 2 points in an 84-92 loss. Thankfully, it turned out my knee injury wasn't serious. Still, the Nuggets made me sit out our final game just to be safe.

The most overwhelming game of the season was our first game against Cleveland. The media built it up as the beginning of the James–Anthony rivalry. It was everywhere. I thought, man, this is just one game. This is crazy. We beat the Cavs both times.

All the comparisons between LeBron and me was a lowlight in my book. I've always been compared to other athletes, at every level. I've never liked being measured by someone else. I didn't like it then and don't now. I realize I'll have to get used to it because, hopefully, LeBron and I are just starting this duel.

On the court, LeBron and I are very competitive. I'll push him, he'll push me back. But off the court it's all love. We're friends and talk often. Our friendship started the night before our first high school game. We sat in the lobby and

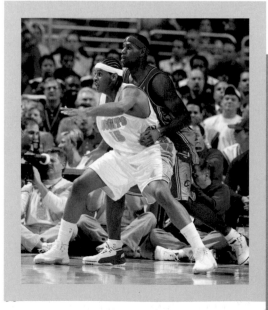

> Believe it or not, LeBron and I are tight.

CARMELO ANTHONY

NBA

GP	FGM-A	Pct	3FGM-A	Pct	Reb	Avg	A	TO	B	S	Pts	Avg
82	624-1,465	.426	69-214	.322	498	6.1	227	247	41	97	1,725	21.0

College

GP	FGM-A	Pct	3FGM-A	Pct	Reb	Avg	A	TO	B	S	Pts	Ave
35	277-612	.453	56-166	.337	349	10.0	77	77	30	55	778	22.2

talked until about 3 in the morning. Whenever we talk we try not to talk about basketball. We talk about life and the things we are going through at the time. We do challenge each other and talk a little trash, too.

LeBron did give me some advice when I made my biggest mistake of the season. It came in a game at Detroit. In the fourth quarter of a 94-75 loss, I heard some teammates grumbling about my shot selection and saying I was shooting too much. I took it too personally. Frustration took over and I refused to go back in the game. I felt everyone was against me. I scored 20 in the first half and childishly thought, OK, let's see what you can do without me.

It didn't take long for me to realize this was a serious rookie mistake. I should not have done that. I had never done anything like that before. The questions from the media came at me left and right in the locker room. The next day I was in a restaurant and I saw my mug shot on CNN. Whenever you see a mug shot of a player it's usually not good news. It blew up all over and had people talking.

I came out and apologized and said I'm not a quitter and that's not me. It was embarrassing. I talked to a lot of friends. LeBron called after he heard about it. First he listened to my side, then he gave me his opinion.

"WHAT HAPPENED, MAN?" HE SAID. HE SYMPATHIZED WITH ME, BUT ADDED "YOU CAN'T DO THAT, MAN." I WAS GLAD HE CALLED. YOU FIND OUT YOUR TRUE FRIENDS DURING ADVERSITY, NOT WHEN EVERYTHING'S GREAT.

People wonder how I felt about LeBron getting the Rookie of the Year award over me. I was happy for him. I called and congratulated him. I expected it, even though our stats were almost identical. The only thing that bothered me was I thought the voting should've been closer given our stats and what we did for our teams.

The spotlight of the NBA isn't easy at any age. And when you hear people criticize your game and your decisions, it wears on you.

I have a problem when I hear negative things said about me. I don't let them go. I start wondering why people would say that. It bothers me, and I start seeing things in a negative light. My mom always tells me to not worry about the doubters. No matter who you are, or what you do, there will be people who will doubt you. I know I have to constantly remind myself of Mom's good advice.

> Two firsts my rookie year: I learned to fly-fish near Meeker, Colorado, and coached star athletes at my first charity basketball game.

I certainly don't get big-headed. Everything has happened to me so fast. My friends and I sit around sometimes and laugh in disbelief.

"Carmelo, we can't believe it's happened to you," they say. "You're on top of the world."

But I don't feel like I am. There are many things I have yet to accomplish. I still feel I have much to prove. My goal is to get better each day.

Two things helped me be successful in my rookie season. I was able to keep it fun, and I rely on a tight circle of trusted friends and professionals.

This first year in the NBA I had fun. I think that's an important thing. If you're not having fun you shouldn't be playing sports. I enjoyed myself.

> Mom gives me a hug, and playing in the NBA gives me much to smile about.

FUN FACT >>> CARMELO WAS ELIGIBLE TO PLAY IN THE OLYMPICS FOR PUERTO RICO, BECAUSE OF HIS FATHER'S HERITAGE, BUT PLAYING FOR PUERTO RICO IN 2004 WOULD PROHIBIT HIM FROM PLAYING FOR THE U.S. IN THE FUTURE.

CARMELO & NICK

Carmelo met Nicholas Owens during a visit to The Children's Hospital in Denver.

Nicholas is 15 months younger than Carmelo and a lifelong Denver Nuggets fan. The two have become friends and have inspired each other.

Nicholas, born with spina bifida, has endured 30 surgeries throughout his life. When he met Carmelo, he was in a 52-night hospital stay. First thing Nicholas wanted to do after being released from the hospital was see the Nuggets play.

"My life hasn't always been easy," Carmelo said. "But it has been no problem compared to what Nicholas has gone through."

On the eve of NBA playoff Game 3 against Minnesota, Carmelo donated $30,000 to Owens towards the purchase of a custom-fitted van for Owens' 300-pound wheelchair.

"I didn't have a choice," Carmelo said. "Nick is someone I care about. I was in a situation where I could help him. My heart told me this was something I had to do."

"What Carmelo has done is very humbling," said Sherwood Owens, Nick's father. "We thank him. It blew us away."

MY ADVICE TO KIDS PLAYING SPORTS IS DON'T WORRY ABOUT WHETHER OR NOT YOU'LL GET TO THE NEXT LEVEL. ENJOY THE MOMENT. HAVE A PLAN AND WORK TOWARD YOUR GOALS. BUT ALSO HAVE A BACKUP PLAN TO FALL BACK ON IF SPORTS DOESN'T WORK OUT.

As I've become more well known, more and more people wanted to latch onto me. "Bay" Frazier has impressed upon me the importance of building my circle. Bay stayed with me in Denver much of that first season to help me with day-to-day things. I've realized my circle was my family and close friends. They are people I trust. Everyone needs a circle for support. You can't do it on your own.

I know times can get hard, even when you are a kid.

If you're saying "Why me? Why do I have to struggle?" If you're feeling like giving up, if you're thinking nothing matters anymore, if you think the odds are against you, I know all those feelings.

Looking back, everything that's happened to me has made me stronger.

You need a strong will to survive. So stay strong. Stay focused.

Don't think about the odds, think about what's possible.

Believe you can be the one to bust out. Believe in a brighter day. Don't listen to the doubters.

Look at each day as a new chance. Don't worry about yesterday, don't worry about tomorrow. Today is the only thing you can change. When you think that way, each day is only the beginning.

CARMELO IN THE COMMUNITY

In October of 2003 I announced a partnership with Family Resource Centers, a nonprofit organization dedicated to family and children's support services.

I decided to partner with this group because I can relate to the people they help, and their goals are very similar to mine. I am very blessed to be paid to do what I love to do, play basketball. I now have the opportunity to help others who are less fortunate than me.

Family Resource Centers assists more than 70,000 people in Colorado with 24 centers in 39 counties. It works with communities to provide services such as early childhood education, parenting and literacy classes and emergency assistance.

If I can make a difference in my community to help people who are struggling, then in the long run, it will make my career more fulfilling.

MELO BAR

In 2004 PLB Sports, a company that helps athletes raise money for charities with fun food products, approached me about making a candy bar with my name on it. When they told me we could help raise money for the Family Resource Centers, I said, "Let's do it."

So the Melo Bar was born February 10, 2004. It's done well, with over 200,000 sold in the first six months. All of my proceeds go directly to the Family Resource Centers. To see all of their products, check them out at www. plbsports.com. You can also find the Melo Bars at my website: www.carmeloanthony.net.

A very Melo Christmas 2003!

> Our first annual "A Very Melo Christmas" party at the Aurora Family Resource Center allows me to meet many kids and their families.

> Our FRC Christmas party produces lots of smiles.

> The Melo Bar raises money for the Family Resource Centers.

BEHIND THE SCENES

Off the court, my first year in the NBA has been a trip.

I was asked to be on some shows, and whatnot. Doors were opened, and I was able to get backstage access to meet many interesting people. I had fun with it. You shake hands, exchange some small talk, and take a picture together. It's cool. You get to see that all these famous people are really just like you and me.

One thing I like to do away from basketball is play jokes on people. The best of 2004 happened after my rookie season.

I woke up one morning and decided: I'm gonna prank everyone in my company... my agents, my lawyers, everybody. I wrote a letter up sayin' I'm firing everybody because they aren't doing their job. So I faxed it to everyone. Then I turned my phone off so no one could talk to me. They didn't know what to think.

Three days later I called them and said I was just kidding.

The thing about joking around with people is they can get you back. My team did just that.

They arranged for me to be on MTV's "Punk'd." The show set me up to think I had to pay for some damages at a hotel. I got a little hot about it because it seemed so real. They got me good. I didn't suspect anything until the cameras came from around the corner and everyone said,

"YOU GOT PUNK'D!"

Oh, yeah, it was fun and everyone had a laugh. I'm willing to laugh at myself. If you dish it, you have to take it.

My team got me back.

> Meeting Special Olympian Kester Edwards (center) and Tim Shriver, the CEO of Special Olympics, at a charity event for Special Olympics I co-hosted with Giorgio Armani.

> Hanging with Tobey Maguire on the set of Spiderman II.

> Late-night host Jimmy Kimmel, Tony Hawk, and me after taping the show.s

Index

Accomplishments
    Fox 45 Player of the Week, 20
    All-Metropolitan Player of the Year, 23
    Baltimore City and County Player of the Year, 23
    Baltimore Catholic League Player of the Year, 23
    McDonald's Boys All-American, 29
    MVP–Paradise Classic, 12
Activities
    BMX biking, 9
    Fly fishing, 41
Baltimore, 4, 14, 19
Baseball, 16
Basketball teams
    Oak Hill Academy, 26, 27, 29
    Towson Catholic Owls, 20, 23
    Syracuse University, 6
    Denver Nuggets, 6
Brooklyn, New York, 4, 8, 10, 12
Coaches
    Darrell Corbett (youth coach), 14
    Mike Daniels (Towson Catholic), 24, 25
    Steve Smith (Oak Hill Academy), 29
    Troy Weaver (assistant coach, Syracuse), 26
    Jim Boeheim (Denver Nuggets), 32
Depression, 24
Detroit Pistons, 35
Education
    Importance of, 15, 16
    Getting good grades, 29
    Going to college, 29
    History, 16
    Mathematics, 16
    Passing the American College Test (ACT), 29
    Spelling competition winner, 15
Family
    Carmelo (father), 8
    Mary (mother), 9, 13, 14
    Michelle (sister), 12
    Wilford (Brother), 8, 9, 20

Family Resource Centers, 46
Friends
    Dontaye Draper, 25
    Tynell Dunkley, 25
    Robert "Bay" Frasier, 3, 25
    Darnell Hopkins, 16
    Kenneth Minor, 25
    Tyler Smith, 25
Hawk, Tony, 47
Health Issues
    Allergies, 13
    Asthma, 4, 13
Injuries
    Eye gash, 9
Kimmel, Jimmy, 47
Los Angeles Lakers, 35
Maguire, Tobey, 47
Madison Square Garden, 31
Melo Bar, 46
"Melo smile", 6
Mount Royal Recreation Center, 19
MTV "Punk'd", 47
NBA Draft, 32
Nicknames
    "Melo", 13
    "Jello", 13
Owens, Nicolas, 43
Players, NBA
    Bryant, Kobe, 35
    James, LeBron, 32, 35, 36
Red Hook Projects, New York, 8, 9
Shriver, Ted, 47
Special Olympics, 47
Statistics, 18, 20, 28, 31, 35, 36, 37, 40
Tournaments
    AAU Tournament, 17
    McDonald's Boys All-American Tournament, 29
    NCAA Final Four, 31
    Nike Extravaganza Tournament of Champions, 29
    Paradise Classic–Red Hook Projects, 12
Window washing, 17

Weblinks

CA 15 - Carmelo Anthony Official Website   www.carmeloanthony.net
Family Resource Centers   www.familyresourcecenters.info
The Melo Bar   www.plbsports.com/cardpages/melo.htm
Denver Nuggets   www.nba.com/nuggets
Syracuse Orangemen   www.suathletics.com/
Reading is Fundamental   www.rif.org